Angels, Demons & Me

LOUISE MAGINNES

First published in Northern Ireland in 2017
by Excalibur Press

This second edition published 2018

ISBN: 978-1-910728-51-2

Edited by
Tina Calder

Cover photo artistry by
Debbie Deboo Photography

Formatting & layout by
Excalibur Press

Excalibur Press
Belfast, Northern Ireland

team@excaliburpress.co.uk
07982628911 | @ExcaliburPress
www.excaliburpress.co.uk

A Message

Shine your light is your natural state.

When you are connected to the inner light within you are connected to the light of the universe where there is more than enough for us all.

Always believe and have faith within yourself, never let another dull your light, keep shining bright, after all that is why you are here on this earthly plane.

..lots of love Lulu x

*To my amazing friend of 24 years and partner of six Jackie,
I love you deeply, your unwavering support and dedication
means the world to me.*

*To my wonderful children Melissa, Lennox, Katie, Troy,
Shawntae, Kiana and Lila Jae for being the amazing people
you are, I love you all with every single breath I take.*

*Thank you to my good friend Rick for all your help and
support physically, emotionally and spiritually, you are a rock.*

*To Dr B, for not just being a doctor but being my earth angel
and supporting me in any way possible. You are the only
woman in my life that I have complete trust in, you've never let
me down. Your straight talking is always a comfort to me
when I need it.*

...I love u all deeply Lulu x

Contents

Introduction

He was a small man and of medium build, I don't remember what he was wearing but I do remember his lovely round face. I was standing on the back of my granda's trailer, it was an exciting day, there was a lot of activity around because we were moving into a new house. There were boxes everywhere. I'll never forget the man's smile, it was like he knew me. I can't really explain it, just that I got a lovely warm feeling as he walked towards me. He stared at me for a few seconds and then he was gone.

Having visions of people around me that no one else saw is one of my oldest memories. I was just three when the lovely man with the warm smile appeared. I'm lucky enough to be able to remember incidences as far back as when I was three years old. That's when the visions began, in the following years the voices too.

Over the next few months I continued seeing children, women and men, all walking past me - but no one else ever saw them. From a young age I spoke very openly about the visions, but it was put down to me having imaginary friends. My 'earth friends' thought I was a nutcase...they still do!

I think I was about eight when I finally realised that others couldn't see what I could, I began to start understanding it all a little bit more then. To be honest I never really cared what others thought or believed because I knew it was my truth and I was confident about that. Over the years I lost friends over it, after all I was the 'weird kid'.

I just simply didn't care what others thought, at night I used to run into my mum or sister's room when I had visions as a young child - those were put down as nightmares and dreams. It was my spiritual awakening at aged 16 that really scared me. My anxiety got worse then and I ended up blowing it all out of proportion in my head at the time. Looking back I realise that it wouldn't have been half as frightening had someone have taken the time to sit down with me to talk to me and realise that I was simply spiritual, not insane.

I was aware from a young age that I could see, hear and feel things that others couldn't, but it would take me many years to fully embrace my gifts. Eventually, when I properly connected with my spirit guides in 1994 at the age of 16 I began to gain a real understanding of how I could use them to help others. When people ask what I do I find it hard to to really define it so that they can comprehend.

For some people I am a spiritual counsellor or I connect with the other side to receive messages from their loved ones or spirit guides to pass on to that particular person or others. In many cases I perform past life regression, as well as removing entities - dark or negative forces - from people or places. As well as that over the years I've found I have an ability to help improve the health and wellbeing of people and animals through energy healing that does not require physical touch. I also have clients who come to me for spiritual guidance or to gain insight about what their future path may hold for them.

For many years I hid my gifts from the outside world, I would tell those closest to me because I couldn't avoid it, but in general whilst I wasn't worried about what people would say I realised it was easier to say nothing because people just did not understand. When I began talking about the fact that I could hear voices to medical professionals they decided that I was suffering from mental illness. At the age of 16, during my spiritual awakening, I was admitted to a mental institution, but I knew what was happening to me was real. Ironically, it was actually "all in my head" but not in the way they thought.

I've spent my life being questioned and ridiculed for what I knew was as real as the sun in the sky. It was my spirit guides who gave me the strength to see past the negativity of those who either refused to believe or couldn't comprehend what I was trying to tell them.

The skeptics out there will have trouble understanding something that isn't physical or logical. They will wonder how I can be so certain there's an afterlife. I can say only, I know what I have seen. Do we question the doctor who diagnoses the patient as having been poisoned? He knows what he has seen. Experience has taught him to recognise the look and feel of poison. Experience has taught me to recognise the other side. There's only a thin veil between the physical world and the spirit world, and the majority of mankind does not possess the psychic sense to see beyond the veil. I'm not the only person on earth with this ability. Throughout history there have been many gifted psychics and seers and there are many living today.

Throughout my life I've been given messages from my guides to pass on to others which I do, and those people are usually grateful for it. Faces appear to me often. Over the years as my gifts grew and expanded I realised that I could actually see where people have pain in their body and I have an incredibly heightened sense of intuition. I know by looking at someone whether they are dishonest or are surrounded by bad energy, within seconds of meeting someone I know whether they are good hearted or not, I know instantly if a person likes me or not and there have even been times when I've seen events happening in places before I even get there.

I won't lie, at times it has been hard to cope, but I'm lucky to have my wonderful partner Jackie, a long time friend of 24 years, who has been at my side for the last six years as I developed, enhanced and began sharing my gifts with more and more people.

I'm a pretty upfront person, aside from the usual number of human flaws, I think I'm pretty easy to get along with. I'm just your average Lisburn girl who talks to the dead. I've always been pretty open about my gifts, I've accepted them now, I suppose you could say I have sort of grown into who I am. When I was younger I wasn't as immediately open, sometimes it was the last thing I would want anyone to know about me. It's only been in the last five years that I've realised how important it was to speak out about it. Now I'm more willing to talk about my abilities and the incredible things I've learned from it.

Going public with my unusual gifts wasn't easy, the questions came in full force. There have been serious questions, silly questions, sad questions, snarky questions and each and every time I have tried to answer them truthfully, patiently...and repeatedly.

I suppose this book is an attempt to answer all the questions I've been asked over the years and to give people an understanding. Most of all, it's to answer the question I get asked the most "when are you going to write a book?" When people asked me this in the past I would change the subject and do my best to avoid the question. After a while I realised it was just easier to write the book than continue to field the damn question.

My main aim with the book is to be as upfront, open and honest as possible. It's not the last book, during my time writing this and working with my editor I realised there was much more to say, it would seem the floodgates have opened and I certainly will follow this up with a more detailed book about my life story and background.

I hope that by reading this book you not only gain a deeper understanding of who I am and how I developed my gifts but that you will also have a better understanding of some of those gifts themselves. This book is about my spiritual journey of healing, self discovery and personal growth. It's about how I began creating a better self, a better life and manifesting my dreams.

I want people to see, from my experience and my view, what I believe happens to us when we cross over from the land of the living to the other side. Maybe some will find comfort in these pages, there might even be a smile or two. One thing I do hope is that this book will encourage others who may have had similar experiences know that they are not alone.

Visions & Voices

Growing up having visions of people became "normal" to me. The striking figures and the voices ended up a comfort in what was otherwise a very stressful childhood for me. When people ask me to describe them it can be difficult because each one is different and each one has a different sensation and feel. During my younger years, and even now, I would regularly see spirits walk past or come to me to pass on messages to other people. Sometimes they were there to warn me of a situation or person I had come into contact with. Much of this though is very private to the people I gave messages to and therefore hard to describe. There are spiritual rules I have to live by which prevent me from talking too much about the details of many of my gifts.

As a young person talking about my visions and auditory experiences wasn't easy. People either laughed and accused me of making up stories or they simply accused me of being mad. Sometimes I was more confident than others talking about them, eventually I didn't care what people thought. The problem was I didn't have anyone to talk to about what I was experiencing, I didn't even know whether what was happening to me happened to other people.

I remember a young girl, I now know her as Jelina, she stood right in front of me and although I was just five years old the image of her is etched on my mind as if it happened yesterday.

Jelina was captivating, she was around 12 years old with beautiful clear skin, piercing blue eyes and red bobbed hair. The first time I saw her I didn't know Jelina would become one of my spirit guides. Dressed in her beautiful white dress that I can only describe as a christening gown, she didn't say anything but her presence made an impression on me that I've never forgotten.

For hours I used to play with Jelina, as the years went on I learned more about her, I believe she is my sister from a former life in 1810. A number of years ago I learned that we had been siblings who were killed along with three other girls, two boys and our parents. At 16 I finally learned she was actually one of my spirit guides.

There has never been one way in which I've felt, seen or experienced a spirit or vision. When I was around eight years old two women just simply walked through the kitchen wall in our hall just chatting away to each other.

I wouldn't say I was ever afraid as such but there were times when I was confused, I didn't know what was happening and couldn't explain it either. Unfortunately, the more I told people, the less they understood and the more I realised I was alone.

By the time I was nine years old I was one of the lads. I was the very definition of a tomboy, anything the boys did, I did. One day I was with my best friend Rod and some other kids, we were attempting to build a treehouse so we were up and down the tree like yo-yos. It wasn't unusual for us to be climbing trees and messing around. But this day was different, that day I remember falling from the tree head first, in a split second I was suddenly standing on the ground with the most beautiful woman I had ever seen. I remember Rod telling me that he saw me doing a roll in mid-air and then slowly drifting to my feet, I have no other explanation than that the woman I met at the bottom of the tree was an angel. She smiled at me and then she was gone.

A few weeks later I was visited again, this time I was in the park with my friend and I fell across a metal climbing frame, it was excruciating, I remember feeling the pain shooting through my body and at one stage losing consciousness. Eventually I was able to pull myself together and I ran home crying to my mum. It was awful, a family friend had to check me out because of how I had fallen and they were worried I would have to go to hospital. I was lying across the worktop and in a lot of pain. Suddenly I was surrounded, I saw seven women, they all looked different and were of different ages, the pain subsided, it just disappeared. I believe they healed me, I believe I was surrounded by angels.

The following year when I was 10 I was wakened from my sleep by a party going on in our house downstairs. There was a lot of noise and singing, I sleepily walked from my bedroom to find out what was going on. A man appeared beside me, he was only about 4ft and was wearing jeans tucked into his boots that looked like they were too big for him. He shuffled across the top of the landing towards my mum's room, he turned around, stopped and stared at me. I was frozen, just watching. Then he did it again, it was very strange. Eventually he just disappeared, he was gone just as quickly as he arrived.

This year was a difficult one for me. A member of my family had threatened me with a knife, I was afraid. She tried to pretend she was joking when another member of my family asked about it but I knew she wasn't, I could see the evil in her eyes, she intended to instil terror in me. That night I couldn't sleep, I was unhappy and had a terrible sense of uneasiness, I couldn't settle myself, the feeling of fear in the pit of my stomach was horrible. Throughout the night I dozed on and off and then something happened that changed my life forever.

As I was wakening from another dozing cycle I heard a faint voice, I tuned in to listen, you know the way you would if someone was telling you something from another room. The voice said to me: "Louise, you are powerful. Keep going and you will see." I wasn't sure what had happened. I thought I was dreaming but I must have fallen asleep shortly after that and when I woke up things were different. The horrible sense of fear and terror had gone. I Felt a lovely warm feeling running through my body and I felt good. I felt positive, and safe.

As I moved into my teens the visions got more significant, over the course of my teenage years I was given many messages, most of which were messages of comfort and reassurance. At the age of 13 I remember walking home on a cold, dark, wet night. Myself and my friend were the last two people in our group to head home. Across the street we saw a woman walking towards us and even though my friend saw her disappear she continued to walk towards me. As she approached me she put her hands on both sides of my arms and smiled. It was a strangely warm and comforting feeling, she rubbed my arms a few times like an older relative might do to comfort you when you're upset, then slowly she was gone.

The woman appeared to us on the street at about 8.30pm and little did I know it wasn't going to be the last time that night. At 11.11pm I was sitting in my bedroom and out of the corner of my eye I saw what almost looked like a mist come and go, the woman was back, she was standing in the middle of my small room. This time I was a little more shocked because I was on my own. I asked what she wanted and why she was there. She simply replied "for you Louise, to guide you through your troubles". I just shook my head, closed my eyes and turned away. I don't know why, I wasn't afraid of her, I think I was just shocked and confused. I remember I tried opening my eyes to look again but she was gone. Although I've never laid eyes on the woman ever since I feel her with me, I know she is still around with me to this day because I feel her warmth.

By the time I was 15 I was truly unhappy. I didn't feel comfortable in the family home, there was always a lot of negativity around, my teens were by far the hardest years of my life. I remember a few days after moving into a new home, I couldn't settle, it felt cold, empty and I felt drained all the time by it. My relationship with my mother wasn't like my friends and their parents. We existed on completely different levels of understanding, we just didn't connect and that caused me a lot of hurt and pain. I could never understand why she was always so hard and harsh on me, she seemed to be overcome with negativity a lot and at a young age I didn't know how to deal with that. In the new house things were as bad as before, mum was berating me in the kitchen, her words cut deep and I felt that in some way, shape or form that I was failing. I didn't know what at, I didn't know what I was supposed to live up to all I knew was that I couldn't handle the negativity I felt was being unfairly thrown at me.

I may have been rebellious in my teens but deep down I was a good girl, looking back I realise that all I needed was emotional security and I felt I never really had that. That day as I stood in the kitchen with my mum I didn't know how to respond, I didn't know how to defend myself or even what I had done to trigger this latest lecture. Then, when I was least expecting it, I heard a voice, it may have been my own voice, say "Louise, block her out. You will have this with certain types of souls. You need to look after your own soul." Three times the voice repeated the message "You need to look after your own soul". I have no memory of what my mum was saying next because I was I was transfixed on the voice and then the an orange light that appeared in the room, three women suddenly appeared standing to my right hand side. I felt them talking to me, there was a sense of ease, I felt safe and from that moment on I knew the negative words my mother said to me would never affect me again.

Negative Energies & Entities

It's easy to make an assumption that when you connect with the other side it's always a positive experience. Certainly that's what most people will want you to believe, and for the most part, it's true. However, just like in life on our earthly plane there are negative forces and entities that can wreak havoc on our lives. In order to be able to recognise these dark forces, or negative energies, I've had to directly experience them in myself. Throughout my journey I've had to learn to identify these destructive forces and be able to not only expel them from my own life but to be able to help release others from their hold.

In recent years spirit removal and the releasing of dark energies and entities from clients has been not only a large part of my work but an incredibly difficult part of my own personal journey. With each client the process is different, we have to work on identifying where the negativity is emanating from and then go through the process of physically, mentally, emotionally and spiritually releasing it.

When I release energy attachments from someone's body they can experience jerk movements, shakes, feeling dizzy or getting the chills and some have been known to be sick. Whilst the initial feeling can sometimes take people by surprise and, in some cases cause concern, within minutes the person begins to feel a lightness around their body and a calmness within.   As they become more aware of their surroundings a bright feeling will come over them. During this process I will re-direct that energy to either where it should be or where it truly wants to be. On the odd occasion the energy, force or entity will attach to me. This usually leaves me with the aftermath of having to do a personal removal on myself sometimes causing me to become heavily exhausted, sick and feeling very drained for a few days.

In August 2016 I had a particularly bad experience. During a removal an entity attached itself to me and unfortunately I felt that I became possessed by it. It's hard to explain what I mean by that because people hear the word "possessed" and they immediately think of the movies but it's not like that. I became quite sick, very nervous and anxious. The good thing was that I knew what was happening, I knew that I couldn't display the fear I was feeling otherwise it could have taken hold permanently. About a week later I was released.

In many cases the removal of an entity or force can take just a few minutes, sometimes it almost looks like there's nothing to it. But for me it often lasts longer. Sometimes I can feel the after effects for days, I've had dark forces take me down with pain for weeks on end, affecting everything from walking and thinking to sleeping. It's not easy, but it's who I am and part of the work I am compelled to do, I'm lucky in that my body, mind, soul and spirit knows how to purge itself now.

A few years back I met Paul, he was an unassuming man,

small in stature with dark hair and piercing blue eyes. I remember his absent warmth when I met him, it was like there were two people struggling to meet me. I soon learned why this was, on hearing just a little bit of his personal journey I was quickly able to understand the seemingly confused man before me.

Paul told me calmly and confidently that he was addicted to heroin, that he had spent more money than he had and not only was his health suffering badly but he was finding it hard to break the connection with the drug. He broke down as he revealed the depth of his addiction - the relationships lost, financial problems and the fact that he was unable to hold down a job having been sacked more than once.

Paul was desperate by the time he came to see me, he didn't know where else to turn. Not just that, he admitted that he was fairly sure I couldn't help him. I sensed deep sadness and remorse in Paul, despite being a heroin addict I was chatting to him in one of his more lucid moments. He admitted to feeling like he was two people, Dr Jekyll and Mr Hyde. On the one hand he wanted to do the right thing and be a functioning member of society but deep inside him he felt an overwhelming urge to escape and heroin was the only thing that would give him that satisfaction.

I had worked with people in the grips of addiction before but something was different about Paul, his inner strength was powerful - everyday he was desperately trying to battle his inner demons and he refused to be beaten by them. The first thing I did with Paul was to discuss what negative attachments and energies were. I explained my understanding from my own experiences.

Although I sensed a deep sadness and remorse from Paul I also experienced a warm, compassionate man in front of me who seemed to have a dark shadow lurking behind him, above him and within him.

I didn't want to alarm him, for some people to hear this can be a difficult process. I asked him to describe some of his negative feelings and within a few minutes he was using analogies such as dark cloud, black shadows and feelings of loss, desperation and a grave sadness that seemed to emanate from the pit of his stomach. This allowed me to approach the subject with ease. Some people don't describe any of these feelings or sensations but Paul was a creative type who finds it easy to talk about his emotions and can eloquently describe feelings with vivid imagery.

Paul had been through a drug rehabilitation programme in the past, and for a time it worked, but the negative entities that had attached to him kept drawing him back to the addiction.
I believe that as a result of Paul's creative and open nature he didn't realise that negative energies were being attracted to him. His own personal energy supply was severely depleted. In my opinion his soul was experiencing a period of weakening.

I worked closely with Paul over a period of time. It wasn't easy. We were both exhausted at times but slowly we worked on strengthening his soul. By helping his soul to recover from its loss we were able to get Paul to the point at which he was able to work with me to remove the various negative energies and entities that were attached to him. I also helped Paul understand better how to protect, cleanse and strengthen himself anytime he felt the "dark mist", as he called it, begin to settle.

Now, three years later, Paul is not just holding down a job but he's pursuing creative endeavours and have been working hard repairing relationships that were damaged during his drug addiction. Paul is a great example of someone who didn't just rely on my work alone, he was willing to do the work, engage in the process and also work to change other aspects of his life in the process.

Over the years whilst trying to understand, or make sense of, what happened to me I spent a lot of time researching how we not only attract negative entities or energies but how they bind to us.

In my personal experience I found that it was always during moments of vulnerability or times when negative emotions were heightened or extreme. Something always triggered a downward spiral. A negative emotion or state of mind would cause a weakening of my soul and in turn negative entities or energies would attach which then of course cause more negative emotions. Getting out of the cycle is often the key, but sometimes the only way to get out of the cycle is to drive the entities or energies away.

I believe that as these negative energies and entities stick to us it begins a process that I call "soul weakening", as our soul is weakened by the negatives it begins to lose the ability to fight them and the cycle begins. For example, some people are able to trace the beginning of their soul weakening to a particular event or period of time. Many identify a lengthy period of feeling angry, while others remember a time of great fear.

I've found that some people who begin on a path of excess drinking, drug use or even gambling end up having entities attach that cause a deep damaging of their soul.

More often than not it can begin with just a little bit of negativity coming from someone we love, whether this is deliberate behaviour, learned or subconscious doesn't necessarily matter because it has the same side effect. If we can't stop ourselves from absorbing these negative entities then it's important to recognise that you may be in a deeply unhealthy relationship and begin to analyse either how you're going to change the negative cycle you're stuck in or extricate yourself from it.

When Amy came to see me she was very reluctant to talk to me. Her sister had heard about me and in a last bid to try and save her sister she pretty much forced Amy to at least meet with me.

Amy was a beautiful girl, strawberry blonde hair, beautiful brown eyes and slender but when she walked into the room she was slouched over like she had the weight of the world on her shoulders. Her eyes were sad and her clothes just hung around her. It was clear she would rather be in a hundred other places than about to sit down in front of me. It took me a couple of sessions to get Amy to open up, to be honest I was surprised she came back each time.

Amy was severely depressed, she eventually told me that out of the blue one day she started feeling suicidal and that she had been self harming for many years. Her confidence was at rock bottom and she blamed herself for everything negative that happened in her life.

For a number of years Amy had been experiencing nightmares, anxiety, mood swings, paranoia and a constant low mood. She refused to take medication, refused to go to counselling and had driven her family to the edge with her constant threats of violence and suicide.

After a few sessions there were no obvious reasons for Amy's behaviour but I sensed a series of negative entities around her. She described a scenario that happened often where she would literally be gasping for air and feeling like she was standing in a crowded room unable to catch a breath. These episodes were always followed by period of a severe low.

I was able to explain to Amy that these episodes were being caused by heightened negative feelings and that if she took notice next time she might find they're triggered by something small such as looking out the window and being annoyed because it's raining or even being irritated by a barking dog in the street. What was happening was each time she had one of these small negative emotions that normally people can deal with, brush off and think nothing of she was opening the door to all those attached negative entities to be able to influence the rest of her day because she had been caught off guard.

It took a lot of work with Amy to get her to recognise her own behaviour and to be able to identify when moments of soul weakening were happening. We worked hard on removing entities and giving her the ability to deal with negative emotions in a more positive way.

Eventually Amy went to her doctor and was prescribed the right medication for her depression, thanks to the work we did together she was able to get the strength to stop self harming and to stop threatening her family. Then when her confidence began to grow she visited her doctor and began taking part in activities she had missed for many years such as swimming and running.

I've found negative entities lurking amongst a plethora of common issues, from pain and being attracted to religious fanaticism to being physically or emotionally abusive to loved ones. I'm not saying that everything negative that happens in our lives is drived by an attachment of a negative entity or energy but certainly for many of my clients we've found that they have felt relief, saw their symptoms dissipate, felt a change in circumstances around them or they've reported feeling completely cured of something that has been annoying them.

Having been the victim of abuse in many forms from physical and emotional to sexual I understand just how damaging it can be when someone breaks through and attaches their negativity to us. I had an ex who would constantly force his negativity on to me. He would emotionally and mentally abuse me by calling me horrific names in a bid to break me. He would tell a lot of lies about me, essentially he would "gossip" about me to people leading them to believe awful nasty things about me. He used it as a tactic to enable people to alienate me and make me think I only had him to rely on.

That's what these people do, they push you into a position where you are completely and utterly reliant and focused on them for everything. You become powerless in your own world and through your loss of self worth comes a deep soul weakening that has a lasting effect.

These "abusers" thrive on making you feel as if you are worthless and if they see a glimmer of vulnerability they will strike, whether it's at home, in a group of friends or within the workplace. In some cases this comes from parents or siblings as well as romantic partners, work colleagues or so-called friends. For children it can result in them growing up with a severe lack of confidence.

One of the most important parts of my work with my clients is working on their self worth and confidence. It's important to help them learn to strengthen their emotions and to own them. Understanding that you have the power to change your world is sometimes the ultimate key for clients to be able to take positive action in all areas of their lives.

Limiting a person's personal and spiritual growth is another way my ex eroded my power over myself, he would lead others to believe I was someone I was not and any time I expressed an interest in things of a spiritual nature he ridiculed and held me back.

I remember a client I had called Helena, she was such a bubbly woman. It was hard to believe she needed help at all. Helena was a typical Northern Ireland mum with a brood of kids who had all flown the nest. Her husband passed away shortly after the youngest child went off to live in America and since then she'd been rattling around in her big house by herself working part-time and volunteering for a local charity. At her most vulnerable point Helena turned to an evangelical church. Feeling like she had something missing in her life she wanted a sense of belonging once again and at the beginning the church was everything she needed.

However, over time she didn't realise she was becoming more and more fanatical about the church, so much so her five children didn't want to visit because they were sick of being preached at. A once liberal woman, Helena began believing things she would never have agreed with when her husband was alive.

After a while she described herself as having turned into a robot. The church could do no wrong. She was giving them most of her money, even going without sometimes just to be seen to be putting money in the basket every week. She was attending class after class, service after service, meeting after meeting.

Eventually Helena began to feel deep feelings of desperation, loss and fear. The church told her it was because she hadn't properly accepted Jesus into her heart. She began locking herself away in the house for fear of "bringing other people down". Her children became very worried.

It was Helena's best friend who first contacted me, worried that she couldn't get through to her friend and worried that the Helena she once knew was gone. It took some clever and accidental meetings to get a session with Helena organised and worse, she believed that what I did was the "Devil's work". But I happened to mention how I felt in my darkest hour to her, something clicked. She started talking.

By our third or fourth session Helena was openly talking about her life and her faith. She's still a Christian but goes to church near her home with her sister in law and friend now. She has a healthy relationship with her faith now and understands the impact of negative entities and works with some of the meditations I gave her alongside her faith. Life has turned around and her five children now enjoy spending time with her.

A lot of people ask me how these energies or entities can attach to us and I believe it's through weakened areas of the aura and soul which creates openings. These openings can often go unnoticed and therefore our subconscious doesn't work to close them or fight off anything that tries to pass through.

The negative energy, force or entity might be just outside a person's own energy field or aura as well. But as a result of a weakening of the aura those negative energies begin to penetrate what is usually a robust and strong outer shell. Some healers and mediums refer to this as "soul loss".

Generally most people don't notice these periods of weakening and, in many cases, don't even feel the effects of a negative entity or energy attaching because their own body, mind and soul works in tandem to fight it off. However, sometimes when our bodies are out of sync or we're going through a particularly traumatic or difficult time we can't concentrate on everything that we should be.

For some of my clients I work on generalised "clearing" of the soul and auras. We work together on building their inner strength and helping them to recognise the signs of attachment.

Energy Healing

When people meet me or find out that I'm an energy healer more often than not the first question they ask is "what is an energy healer?". The best way I know how to answer that is to explain that everything that surrounds us is made up of energy. From our physical bodies to our existence on a spiritual, mental or emotional level, everything is connected via energy streams. More often than not our natural healthy vibrations become out of sync or are negatively affected by the world around us. What I do is help people regain a sense of balance in their energetic circuits enabling them to utilise and implement their natural healing capabilities.

There are several methods and disciplines for practising energy healing, however, rather than practice just one type, over the years with assistance from spirit, I have developed my own style that has proven very effective for my clients.

Most of my life I've known I had a healing ability, however, it took me a while to realise just how important this was. As a child I would always gravitate towards animals, especially those that were sick. I always knew instinctively when they were sad or sick and I knew that there was something different about my hands compared to the other children I knew. I have a very vivid memory of a time when my own dog was sick, I knew he was dying and my body went into big jerk movements, I felt his pain, I couldn't stop crying. At that moment I wasn't crying because my dog was dying, I was crying because I felt every strike of pain he felt and it was excruciating.

Although I was a typical tomboy growing up there was another side to me, when I wasn't playing outside with the boys there was a real nurturing side to me, I loved playing with my dolls, to me they were my babies. I loved looking after them. It's no surprise I'm a mother of seven children now. I think this side of my personality was developing to give me the ability to eventually become an energetic healer. I was always empathic, I couldn't just understand the pain and suffering of others, I felt it.

When I perform a healing, I can tell where on a person's body they are sore. I'm not sure why I started this but in the last three years when I'm speaking to people I naturally scan their body with my eyes, in a matter of seconds I know everything about their health. When I'm performing a one-on-one session and I scan the body with my hands I can instantly tell what operations a person has had or may need, when I come to a problem area on the body my hands heat up or go cold and tingle, that's what helps me to tune into the problem.

On scanning someone things can appear to me in different ways, one common way is that I see a person's aura changing in colour or have certain colours concentrated in one place. It's hard I have a certain set of rules that I live by and whilst I instinctively know what different colours or visions mean, it's not something I could teach or explain. For example when I see three colours together white, black and grey I know that someone is battling mental illness. It see it from the shoulders upwards and I can tell where the pain or trauma is emanating from. Whilst certain colours will depict certain things for me the strength of the colour and intensity will also help me to know the strength of the trauma or pain.

When I connect to someone I feel like they do, I connect with their emotional state so if they are sad I become sad, if they are sick then I begin to feel it. Even if someone around me has a sore head, I feel it. I keep my circle around me very small, it's a way of protecting myself because I do all my own healing as well. Something I've done a lot of is energy healing with pregnant women. I am usually also able to tell whether or not the mother has had or is likely to have complications during the course of her labour. In many cases I can alleviate fears or encourage them to get something checked out to give them peace of mind. One of the things I've proved I'm able to do time and time again is tell someone the sex of their baby before it's born.

When it comes to energetic healing a person doesn't need to be around me to feel the effects. We are all souls on an earthly plane and I am able to connect and work across great distances.

At home I even make my own mixtures when the children are sick. Whether it's a cold or flu it's usually gone within two days, we're very lucky my children are rarely sick and I put it down to me being able to help their bodies fight sickness before it takes hold. I believe since 2013 I've healed thousands of people. I've connected with people's loved ones to help reassure them and settle the grieving process. I've connected with many dark entities and lost souls. I always have energies around me, they've even been caught in our home on CCTV.

When I was just starting out to explore whatever abilities I had in relation to energy healing I attended a healing ministry in County Tyrone in 2014 but something didn't sit right with me. I spent three nights with them and I felt there was something insincere about what was happening. It was very over-dramatic and theatrical, she was flopping about like a fish on the floor "removing" demons I remember standing being completely dumbfounded by it. My experience was completely different, I felt that she was playing it up and maybe being far more dramatic for effect. As far as I was concerned that wasn't how spirit worked and I didn't believe people should be paying for a "show" when they just wanted healing. Needless to say I left and never returned. Something similar happened with a circle I became involved with in Belfast. After three weeks it just didn't resonate with me, it wasn't how I connected with spirit and I couldn't understand why people were being told to "use your imagination". It wasn't long before I realised that I needed to go on the journey alone and since I made that choice I have been much happier.

People always ask for examples of the "healing" I do and it's hard to talk about them because in many cases it's a very private matter between myself and the person I am working with. However, there was an incident when we were moving in slow traffic and I saw a lot of people standing around a car. Suddenly I saw the soul of a little boy rising from the crowd. I told my partner Jackie to stop the car and I ran to the crowd. I quietly connected with the energy of the little boy who was just four years old and guided his soul back towards his body. He eventually was left only with a broken leg.

Using My Senses

Throughout my life I've had extremely heightened senses. I see, feel, hear, taste, smell and experience things at a level some people would have difficulty processing. Over the years it's left me feeling confused, powerless and caused me a great deal of pain and suffering as I learned to cope with the complete sensory overload that I would regularly be faced with. However, over the years I've been able to harness each of my six senses as well as listen to my intuition and inner guidance as well as find ways to deal with the negative effects and embrace the positive aspects of being an empath. During my work I utilise my ability to be able to put myself into what I can only describe as a trance.

During my self induced trance states I find myself traveling through a tunnel within my thoughts. I'm traveling forward at first then up and down. Around the tunnel there are images that seem to be alive, I see people, some are waving me forward while others are crying out for my help. I seem to be able to control my speed but the faster I move I seem to bypass the outer darkness. When I travel slow and descend I pass through different areas and emerge into a bright light, it's like waking up into my thoughts where I have existed all along. An Angel appears before me telepathically asking me what I need to know? I give the name, and place of birth of any individual soul I need information on, the Angel looks into what I believe to be the Book of Life and passes that information on to me past, present and future. The Angel says the Book of Life is here to help make us better people. Usually moments later I wake up back in my physical body.

When I'm in a trance state, I usually sit quietly gazing into the realms of the spirit world, the ability for me to see the other side is an important part of my work. However, as well as that a great deal of my time is spent concentrating on this life and the issues people have in the here and now.

Probably the first time I really consciously experienced going into a trance was in my childhood. I was just nine years old when I believe I had my first trance mediumship experience. We had been heading on a family holiday to Blackpool via the Liverpool boat from Belfast. During the trip my father gave me a new pink and black watch, I was completely fascinated by the second hand, so much so that I became totally transfixed watching it go around. It wasn't long before I became aware that my surroundings were changing as I kept focused on the watch. The light in the cabin changed from its usual yellow/white glow to a very dull, almost sepia colour and the smoke from my mother's cigarette was turning from a silvery mist into an amazing orange colour.

Suddenly my family looked like negatives of themselves. My head was down, looking at my wrist, but somehow I was also standing in a room that was familiar to me. I was watching my best friend Alex (name has been changed) standing over a bed where her mother lay looking very sick indeed. I heard her say

"That's enough now" and Alex was led out of the room by someone taller than she was.

Back in the cabin of the boat, my mother was asking me what I was looking at and forcing me to answer her, my brother and friend were making up funny songs and my father was half asleep with his head hanging to one side. Yet I could still see Alex, she was holding a beautiful red coat in her hands, only now she was in a dim sepia-colored light and her father was telling her not to cry. The following week I wanted to go to Alex's house with a gift I'd bought her in Blackpool, but my mother said I shouldn't go. She explained to me that Alex's mother had died the week before and I should wait till another time to give her the gift. Two days later I saw Alex, we had been talking about her mum and she told me that she had seen her two days before she died and that her mum had given her the coat (which she still has to this day). That was at about 6pm, the same time I went into my trance on the boat on the same day. For me, this was the beginning of what I now know to be trance mediumship, where my mind "moves out" to allow a spirit being to use my mind and body to communicate with their loved ones. During one of these trance states my mind becomes clear and still, sometimes my eyes are closed sometimes open. I experience a change of light and tone around me. Often when this occurs I sense my awareness separating into two parts, and while being able to stay in the moment, I am equally aware of being somewhere else and can describe, in full detail, both situations. Not only can I receive messages in my mind from the other side, through mental mediumship, but I can also enter a trance and allow my mind and body to be used by a spirit person for more direct communication.

Another similar experience which was much darker linked me with a neighbour that had sexually abused me from I was nine years old right through until I was 12. One day when I was in the street I noticed the Police and an ambulance crew at his home. I tentatively walked down the street towards the commotion. Within a few minutes I saw him being carried out on a stretcher, all I could see were his feet, he was covered up otherwise. As they put him into the car I suddenly felt my body going into a shut down, I felt tightness around my throat like I was choking and I couldn't breathe, my insides felt like they were falling out, I ran home screaming, it's so vivid in my memory. Then I found out he had taken his own life by hanging and I realised that I had been experiencing what he did.

For me using and embracing the senses is a vital part of the work I do in order to be able to connect with or tune into an energy. I have to be open with all my senses. Most people can see, touch, smell, taste and hear the things that happen on this earthly plane but it's important to open your other channels of communication not only to listen to the other side but to be able to truly listen to yourself. By allowing all your senses to work together in energetic harmony it becomes easier to connect and communicate with those no longer here. Unfortunately, opening all your channels of communication can leave you vulnerable to energy vampires and soul drainers who seek to extract every ounce of energy you possess without ever replacing your supply. There are many energy vampires who are unaware of their actions, just being in their company can be exhausting.

My ex was an energy vampire. However, he knew exactly what he was doing. Not only did he use sex to control me but he also used it to deplete my energy and find ways of attacking my self confidence and self worth whilst doing it.

Normally in a healthy sexual relationship both people are giving and receiving energy on an equal level. Both people fully open their hearts and souls to let the other person in. But when a vampire is involved the relationship is all take, take, take and the person giving is left feeling used and exhausted physically, mentally, emotionally and spiritually.

It's always worth taking stock of you own personal energy supply and how you feel within yourself if you think you might be in a relationship with a vampire.

Mediums, Psychics & The Afterlife

A lot of the work I do with clients has a basis in my capabilities both as a medium and a psychic, Interestingly these terms are almost interchangeable in popular culture, however, the reality is that they are two very different gifts which are often used in a variety of ways. So what is the difference? A medium is a psychic, but a psychic is not necessarily a medium. Someone who is just psychic can give you a prediction, but they can't tell you where or who they got it from. I, and other true mediums, not only can tell you what is going on and what will happen, but we can tell you who on the other side is bringing the message.

Of course it's impossible to broach the subject of mediumship without discussing or being curious about life after death. For many the idea that there is an afterlife is perfectly plausible but asking them to believe that someone may be communicating with the other side is a whole other story. For me it's not a strange concept. Seeing, feeling and speaking to the other side has been a perfectly normal part of my life since childhood.

I don't think I can say exactly when I really started communicating properly with people who had passed over but it was definitely from when I was a small girl. At that time it wasn't really like having a conversation, I just knew things. I understood so little at the time. One of my earliest memories of this was walking home one day when I was about seven years old and realising that someone very special was going to be taken from us. As I was walking into my back garden, I 'heard' the other side, although I didn't know at the time that's who was communicating with me. I can't recall the exact words I heard, I'm not even sure it was a full sentence. Nevertheless, I knew what they meant and I remember it like it was yesterday. Other messages like this one came to me at other times. The effect of these messages, for me, helped to ground me. Even if I didn't like what I'd been told, the fact that I'd been told these things in advance eventually helped me gain perspective.

I feel now because I have such a close relationship with my spirit guides, and also because I've had more than one out of body experience myself that I have a good understanding of what happens to us when we die. Although I acknowledge that many people have experienced different things I find that being able to communicate my understanding of it to my clients has very often brought them a real sense of ease, especially those dealing with loss and grief.

I've heard all manner of questions on this subject, people are naturally curious, they have fears, they've heard about going into the light and want to know everything from does it hurt and whether we lose our memories to whether or not everything we had before is there when we cross over. All I can tell them is what I have heard from the souls on the other side who have told me that when we die we leave either through our feet or the top of the head. Some people talk of a "silver cord" that attaches each person to their life here on earth but this isn't something I've ever discussed with the other side nor is it something I have any knowledge of. When we pass on to the other side there are various things that people feel, from floating and flying to walking or gravitating towards the light, whilst it's different for each person there are a lot of similarities. There's a feeling of anticipation - maybe in some cases a little fear, but more anticipation. Nothing at all is forgotten. In fact, whereas now we can only remember some highlights of our life, on the other side we remember everything.

I believe that after physical death our spirit and soul sever the body traveling through a tunnel effect into the fourth dimension back into our spirit body, we then wake back up into our thoughts where we have existed all along. There are those around us that we know, some may have been friends or relatives who passed on before us, and others may be souls that do not incarnate with us but with whom we share a genuine connection. I believe at this stage we don't notice all the souls around us, only those with whom we have shared experiences. It is in the spirit world we review in detail the life we have lived in the earth realm. We see the possibilities of all the choices we didn't make. We review our life in the three dimensional world three times. After review a healing takes place so that we can move on. Death is just another form of life.

In terms of my own psychic abilities I always knew what was

going to happen next but more often than not those around me just brushed it off as nonsense. I would have liked to have been able to confide in my mum about how the gifts really made me feel, but it wasn't easy, she was a controlling woman. For some reason she had a negative energy about her, it meant I would feel uneasy around her sometimes and unable to open up to tell her things. It would upset me that when I did think I could open up and told her of something that I saw or knew she would laugh and say I was "stupid". It was how she coped with how I was. She regularly put us down when she was consumed with negativity. She would try to combat this by having what I call a "show boat" home, everything was perfect, we were in the best clothes and people would see our perfect lives. But my life wasn't perfect, I was crying out to connect mentally and emotionally with her. Ironically I look back and wonder how I was able to deal with it all and then realise it has made me a much stronger person today.

Of all the things I have predicted over the years not one hasn't come true. I've even been contacted by mediums in America to help them with cases they are working on. I even have crows that will circle around me to warn me of certain things. When I was about 7 or 8 I was out playing on my roller boots and I went flying down a hill, at the bottom was the lemonade van coming towards me and I went smashing right into the van which they believe was going at about 35mph. The driver, in shock, jumped out and dragged me out from under the van, he was in a terrible state but I didn't have a mark on me. I ended up telling him that everything was ok. Then I said to him "it's fine, your mum Betty said that was close".

With an even more shocked look on his face he exclaimed "What? My mum is dead!". I calmly told him that I knew because she was standing to my right and the colour just drained from him. Another incident that happened when I was hanging around with my friends at the local school one evening and out of nowhere I saw one of the boy's dad's falling off step ladders. They lived just facing the school. Of course being a kid he just laughed at me and said "yeah, whatever". Sadly, about a week later that's exactly what happened and he lost his dad.

I also remember about a month after my 16th birthday I was messing about with my friends and fell and hit my head, according to my friends at the time i was out cold for a few minutes. They were worrying and crying, back then we didn't have mobile phones, so some of them ran off to a house nearby and got the man to come and help. They were in a complete state of panic. For me it was a magical experience. I saw me having a baby a little girl, I saw what she looked like, I felt a lot of happiness and sadness and I was told that it would happen on the 18th of October. I even saw the room, hospital, doctor, midwife, everything. Every little detail was so clear to me, it was as if I was actually there. The following year I gave birth to my eldest daughter Melissa on the 18th of October 1995. In the coming years this wasn't unusual. I started having many visions about pregnancies, births, dates and more.

In recent years there was an incident where myself and Jackie, my partner, were driving down the M1. Out of nowhere I started feeling really sick, it completely encompassed me, I was filled with dread and sadness. I knew what had happened, in my heart I just knew. There was no evidence on the motorway, the lanes were clear, traffic was moving smoothly and to anyone driving along nothing would have been suspicious. I turned to Jackie and explained that I knew we were driving towards a really bad crash ahead. He knew I was telling the truth, he'd experienced my premonitions and predictions many times so we approached the rest of the motorway with caution. As we got further up the motorway we arrived at what I can only describe as a horrific pile-up. The emergency services were in attendance and there were numerous cars and people involved. It's not easy knowing these things, but I know I am given this information for a reason. Maybe on occasions like this it's merely a way for the other side to confirm that what I do see is real, relevant and important.

It took me years to shine my own light, to develop my gifts and accept who I really was and what my purpose was. It was a tough journey for me, I had to learn to listen to my "self" and "spirit". Unfortunately, for many years I was surrounded by negativity from a variety of sources and that weakened my ability to progress my gifts. Once I had broken away from these negative influences I found that I became stronger and in turn so did spirit. I am who I am now because I listened. When people read this book I want them to understand that this is my journey, this is how I came to be where I am today with my gifts and what I do. Not everyone's journey will be this way but for those who are on a difficult path I want them to know that they aren't alone and that no matter what anyone says they should try to bring their gifts to light and to live their light.

It's hard to find ways to explore, develop and understand their experiences, however, it concerns me that people spend a lot of money doing courses and workshops and training in spiritual practices. I think that some people are charging too much for the support and training they give and it's unfair on the people who are trying to learn what to do with their gifts. Similarly I feel that charging a lot of money for individual readings and sessions is also excessive. I worry about how greed can affect the readings. Greed is negative energy and if something is being tainted by that I believe it's not as effective. My personal motto is that if you own it, it will own you. However, if you share it, it will return to you.

Protecting Myself & Others

I've found over the years that protecting myself is one of the most important rituals I have to go through; both for myself and my family. I never want to be in a position where the negativity I deal with or soak up affects how I am. It's so important to remember that if you are sensitive like me, negativity from others is easily picked up. This seems to happen more when you are feeling low, or when you can sense hostility from others. I'd like to share a prayer that I use every day for protection. I say this prayer daily. Please try it for yourselves.

"I am grounded by the light of the Divine as it surrounds me and enfolds me with light and love. I am protected as I am watched by the Divine day by day, night by night. The presence of the Diving makes me safe, secure and protected."

Always in my work as a healer and spiritual guide, I am careful, I have to ensure that I cannot be overcome. That might sound like a very strong statement but at times the negativity would consume me if I didn't constantly keep an eye on it. Sometimes people can act flippant when it's talked about, but if they had to deal with it themselves they wouldn't feel that way. I think that to be sensitive is to be strong at the same time. Part of being strong is self protection when it's needed. My journey to realising how important self protection is hasn't been easy. They say sometimes you have to learn the hard way and I guess that might be the case with me.

Looking back across my life and my experiences I see now that I went into emotional meltdowns regularly for a number of years. It was a difficult time for me. I feel like my personality was all over the place. I was a normal, mad teenager full of cheek but still loving, and craving love in return. As an adult looking back I probably should have listened to those emotions as and when they were happening. Maybe there were signs for me to see. Lessons to learn but I was so out of balance and lost. I think recognising those signs would have been difficult for me.

I had my first child when I was just seventeen. It was around this time that I began to literally feel others people's pain. Everything was changing for me spiritually. My awareness seemed to take a sort of jump. I began hearing voices and had very strong intuitive feelings about people speaking positively or negatively about me personally. I just knew the score with others feelings towards me. It was uncanny. Even though I was a single mum at this time; I intuitively knew I would meet someone two years later. Sure enough I did, and also in the exact place I had visualised our meeting happening years before. I was having many vivid dreams and hearing children giggling and people talking quite clearly when others with me couldn't hear anything.

I was always acutely aware of everything around me, I started slowly to take note of the things I was being told by the other side and eventually I realised that I wasn't the only one protecting me. As I was learning I had help. I was 19 when I had my second child Lennox. The night he was born I was lying there looking at him as we lay in the hospital ward together. There was a stillness around, it was quiet and peaceful. I knew we weren't alone and I could sense the presence of seven women who were standing around my son Lennox. They were smiling and the feeling of peace that washed over me was unreal. One of the seven women put her hand on my stomach. I was discharged the following day.

Within a couple of days of being at home I started to feel really ill and before long was on the way back to the hospital. They told me that my afterbirth hadn't been removed properly and I had to stay for another procedure. I often wonder about whether or not when the woman placed her hand on my stomach was she telling me what had happened? When I was coming back round after the procedure I saw the same seven women standing around me in the theatre. The same feeling of peace returned and any anxiety, worry or feelings of being unwell were lifted. My connection with these seven women had begun and I met them again after my third child Katie was born a year later. After seeing them for the third time I called them 'my seven grandmothers'.

The following years weren't going to be easy for me. My partner at the time was an extremely negative man, as a result of his behaviour he caused me a significant amount of anxiety and trouble. I experienced a significant amount of loss, I felt like I couldn't think, let alone connect with my previously

Angels, Demons & Me

growing spirituality. I lost some of my interests and disappeared into depression. It felt like being in the pits of hell and I had no control over my moods and feelings. Negativity had taken over and I think now it has helped me realise how important self protection is. I began to realise how important it was for me to clear negative people out of my life, I had to learn not to tolerate anyone who wasn't supportive. I suppose you could say that I had almost entered a self preservation phase of my life and in the most basic way had begun self protection.

By 2013 I had had my seventh child, Lila-Jae . Fifteen days after giving birth I went to bed for a lie down. I knew that I had come out of my body and that I was travelling through a tunnel. I was aware of others around me when this was happening. They were crying and trying to grab at me. I saw the most horrible things during these moments. All of a sudden I found myself in the most beautiful place I've ever seen. I can't describe how beautiful it was. I could hear a voice, I moved towards it because I instinctively knew I was going to be given information. I was told that I ignored what I had been told in March 2002. All of the information made sense to me as I recalled my life back then. I was told I wasn't ready to receive the messages. The moments passed quickly and I found myself back in my body again, lying on the bed in my room. It all seemed very clear at that point; I was meant to focus on helping others. I had to share my gift with others.

Whilst we can protect ourselves to ensure dark or negative energies don't attach we often have the situation that we need to remove them in the first place. I personally don't believe that passive removal techniques such as lighting candles, meditating or doing spells will remove a negative energy or entity. In my experience they have to be forced to leave with an energy stronger than theirs. This means I have to do a lot of work on myself to ensure that I can keep myself at a strength level that can cope with or deal with those entities. When performing a removal I have to be careful to expel it in the right direction and to ensure that not only is it removed in the right way but that both myself and my client are protected properly.

In my opinion, anyone who charges more than thirty pounds to do this type of work is out just to make money. I fully believe in Spiritual Law which basically guides me in the direction of acceptance in the form of donations, therefore I don't have a price list and people can choose whether to donate or not, I don't expect it from them because I want to make my gifts accessible to everyone and I trust that spirit will look after me. Obviously nowadays spirituality is talked about freely, people can take multiple courses in all sorts of subjects and they want to quit their day job and help others. We all need money to live, but I don't agree with some of the high charges being placed by some in order to take advantage of people who may be fragile or vulnerable. Especially if a dark entity has attached themselves to that person. If someone like myself has a spiritual gift, that gift should be used to help others and people should feel they can approach me any time. I suppose in a way I feel it's my duty to educate people in order for them to be protected from those who would take advantage of their vulnerability.

The Energy Of Words

When it comes to how we use our energy one of the most important things, in my opinion, that we have to be mindful of is the energy contained in our and how we use them. As we know, everything around us contains a specific energy signature, vibrating at a different rate. Even we have our own vibrational rate. I believe that people who experience the spiritual side of life vibrate at a higher rate than those who are closed to it because the spirit world exists in a higher rate of vibration than our three dimensional earth plane. At night our spirit breaks from this plane and goes into spirit world, I've never believed that we have to die to visit the other side, by tuning into our spiritual energy I know that we can communicate with those who have passed into the spirit realm.

As a result of the importance of energy in our existence I firmly feel that being careful about how we utilise and express language both internally and externally is vital. With each word or set of words we create a different energetic path. For example, when going through a rebirth the phrase "I AM" becomes a crucial part of the process, especially when linked to a healing. Using the phrase "I AM" can be a very powerful tool when setting your own goals and intentions. It allows you to create the energy of your end goal rather than the energy that keeps you stuck in the position you want to get out of.

Using the phrase "I AM" can be as simple as saying - and believing - phrases such as "I AM healing, I AM healing myself", "I AM successful in my career" or "I AM a healthy, happy person". By using "I AM" in these types of phrases, mantras or in conversation you are simply calling to the universe to let it know that you truly believe that what you're asking for is not only possible but happening in the present. When I am doing a session with someone the use of "I AM" is key to what we do together. I always start with a meditation myself and when I connect to spirit I say "I AM ready to heal this person".

Many people ask me who or what "spirit" is for me, assuming that I don't believe in the traditional Christian God. For me it's not about believing in church, bible or religion as a doctrine but rather belief in a higher power. This doesn't mean I don't believe in God, from what I know Jesus was just a healer, someone who must have used energy to heal people. I remember once going to a circle in which a woman believed she could teach people to be spiritual, thing is I don't believe you can teach it to someone, I believe someone is either born that way or they embark on a journey or rebirth at some point in their life that gives them the ability to connect. This woman actually questioned by ability to be spiritual, ironically I found her use of language to be very energetically negative. She believed someone couldn't be spiritual and use profanity, she believed people had to be 100% positive at all times. I'm more realistic. We're only human after all and we come with our imperfections, it's what makes us who we are. Welcome to the real world, yes - we should aim to be as positive as we can as much as we can but no one should ever use their language to make others feel like a failure just because they've felt crappy or a bit negative - it's called 'life', it's called being human.

It took me years to clear away negativity built up in me over years of hearing negative words from people, I used to absorb it, every single last word that was armed with darkness and it had a profound effect on me over time. Now it's a different story, now I know how to redirect those words back to the person saying them and if I'm honest I don't feel guilty about sending their own negativity back to them because they have to learn to dissipate and eradicate their own dark thoughts the way I had to. I worked hard over the years to reduce and remove that negativity from my life, I've no intentions of ever absorbing it again from another person.

The Importance Of Meditation

Meditation is incredibly important to me on a daily basis, it helps to focus my mind and be able to tune into the spirit realm in advance of meeting a client. Taking time out to meditate can help us re-evaluate and analyse not only our past decisions but our future actions. It can act as a force of regeneration that helps us to rebalance our energies. Taking time out each day to work through whatever issues might be going on in your life will not only work to your own benefit but also to the benefit of others around you. By being able to acknowledge the issues those around you may be facing and to understand how we are all inextricably linked psychically, emotionally, mentally and physically it becomes much easier to share your life and this earth with everyone else around you.

Every day I meditate for around 30 minutes and for the same amount of time before a connection as well. As well as that throughout the day I will meditate at other intervals for a moment or two at a time. People think that you have to sit still and "ummm" and "aaaah" for hours to achieve true balance but I don't. Meditation is just a way for you to bring yourself back to your higher self. I started meditating properly when I was about 26 and it's played a big part of my spiritual life ever since. The meditation back then began for me after what I now know to was an out of body experience not long after I had my sixth child Kiana. I had been lying on top of my bed stressed out and went into a trance and despite seeing many things and experiencing things I hadn't before I learned that night the importance of meditation and I've done it every day since. I truly believe it is good for the mind, body and soul. Not only does meditation help to relieve fear but it slows down our over-active minds and helps us focus on what is truly important to us.

During the meditation process I find this a great time to acknowledge my own beliefs, connect with my spirit and to analyse my choices against my own ethical or moral beliefs. When analysing the choices I've made and the choices ahead of me I try to gain an understanding of the circumstances that may have led me to where I am which helps me to reinforce the foundations that I've built my life on. Our minds are like gardens, whatever we put in there will grow and flourish. If you put negativity in there then it will spread like weeds, put positivity in there it will bloom like a beautiful garden in spring time.

It is during these times of meditation that I can truly connect to me, a lot of people spend this time trying to emulate someone else but this is the perfect time to learn how to be yourself. Being connected to yourself allows us to become grounded, once grounded and confident in our true self we can then see with our hearts, see what is truthful, accept it and be truthful. Connecting with our truth allows us to grow and move forward.

During times of meditation being passionate about our

intentions is more likely to effect change. This is why many people believe strongly in the power of thought. For many people who have been able to make the transition from automatic negative thought processes to a more positive one, the changes in their lives have been described by many as miraculous. Something so small can totally change a person's complete outlook on life and in turn affect almost all areas of their life. To believe everything is possible is to create a reality where you can achieve anything.

There are times, however, when meditation isn't enough or when a person doesn't want to embark on a lifelong journey of self-discovery. More often than not these people would come to me when they have experienced soul loss. In my experience basic meditation, positive thinking, yoga or other spiritual practices performed alone will not repair the damage caused by soul loss. When someone feels disempowered they often need guidance and counselling that can help them to work through each of the phases of repairing their soul. I find that for many of my clients, especially those who don't have friends and/or family who understand their journey my presence, support and guidance helps them to much more fully commit to what they need to do to bring themselves back into spiritual balance.

Here is a meditation you could try at home to begin the process:

Sit or lie in a comfortable position, close your eyes and breathe slowly. Concentrating on your breath until all sounds around you fade into the background.

Once you are in a comfortable position slowly imaging your entire body being immersed and surrounded with a bright white light.

Using the power of sapphire light change the colour from bright white to sapphire.

As the colours change back and forward as you "feel" you need concentrate on areas of your life and body that you feel need healed, calmed or rebalanced.

When you feel calmer, more peaceful and lighter allow both colours to merge within and around you.

Feel your body becoming the light as it changes colour.

Finally say "Here, I am home", repeat the word "home" or the phrase until you experience a rush throughout your body as you become balanced and energised.

Patience & Timing

Throughout my journey I've had a wide range of experiences, some positive others negative, however, one thing they all have in common is that I've learned something new each time both about my gifts and more importantly about me. For years I was lost, I was searching for something, I didn't know what. I tried everything to fill the gap in my soul. I dabbled with religion, I played the marriage game and I signed up for one course after another as I desperately searched for something that was within me all along. 2002 and the birth of my fourth child Troy was one of my many turning points.

During my pregnancy I was very ill and whilst I was giving birth I had an out of body experience. I was suddenly watching myself from above as I was having my son. I remember asking and begging to return to him and a voice said to me "Yes, you can return Louise because you have work to do". I couldn't tell if the voice was male or female, I was surrounded in pure white smoke, it was an amazingly peaceful feeling. This year was transformative for me, communication with the spirit realm became possible, my understanding, clarity, visions, insights and awareness began to increase and my connection to the other side became stronger.

Now I am privileged to live in two realms, the human realm and the spirit realm. For years and years I tried to make things happen with no success, what I learned that year was that only patience and the right timing will reveal our true purpose. It might sound like a cliche but for anyone, who like me has been searching for guidance, it will come when you least expect it, overnight everything can change and what you felt was once not possible can become possible as you awaken. When the time is right the doors will open for you, as they did for me, and you will experience your awakening and begin to live and love to the full whilst experiencing this earth and universe very differently. When it happens just go with the flow.

Today I live by the rules of the spirit world There are many things I don't reveal because spirit has asked me not to and I feel I must respect them. When people come to me for a healing I ask them to close their eyes because I feel it's the best way to for me to adhere to spiritual law and allow them to be fully in the moment. I believe I answer to a higher power. I work on the basis of spiritual law by the power of three. When I connect to spirit I will ask three times for spirit to answer what I need. Three is an incredibly powerful number, for some it represents "all" and for others it is the number of the whole because it contains the beginning, middle and end.

One thing that I feel makes me unique is that I will always be 100% honest with people about the messages that come to me no matter how much I dislike knowing the information. I feel that no matter how hard it is for me to communicate these messages that I have to respect both my client and spirit. I don't like some of the predictions I get either but equally there are many wonderful joyous messages that warm the heart,

In writing this book I wanted to convey to you, my reader, is that it's not easy thinking, feeling and acting positively at all times. Feeling a bit crap, being a bit down or even depressed is not abnormal so we should never beat ourselves up for having down days. Don't allow your own expectations of yourself or others of you make you feel like a failure. Sometimes we all need a little help to see the light shining between the trees. The important thing is that you always keep your eye on that glimmer of light in the distance.

A Letter To You

This is to those of you who have had a rough week, month, year. You may feel that you are weathering many storms and as a result you may have lost faith and/or feel invisible.

There are those of you who may not know how much more you can take and you blame yourself for all that has happened around you.

Please know that you are incredible, you make this world a good place just because you are you, you have so much potential and so much more to do with your life. Keep hanging in there because good things are always on their way.

..lots of love Lulu x

About The Author

Energy and spiritual healer Louise Maginnes, aka Lulu, grew up in Lisburn, Northern Ireland where she lived with her parents and three siblings.

Born in 1978, life growing up was tough for Louise. Like many people who have come through difficulties in their childhood, Louise hopes that her story will be an inspiration for others who may be experiencing similar situations to those she has courageously battled through herself.

For some people she is a spiritual counsellor, someone who connects with the other side to receive messages from their loved ones or spirit guides to pass on to that particular person or others.

In many cases she performs past life regression, as well as removing entities - dark or negative forces - from people or places. As well as that over the years Louise has found she has an ability to help improve the health and wellbeing of people and animals through energy healing that does not require physical touch. She also has clients who come to her for spiritual guidance or to gain insight about what their future path may hold for them.

Angels, Demons & Me is Louise's first autobiographical book which details her extraordinary journey on her path to becoming a spiritual/energy healer. Inside Louise allows the reader to delve into her own past whilst creating awareness for the range of abilities she has been gifted and developed over the years.

The story brings the reader close to mother of seven Louise as she reveals what led her life to the point of writing about her challenging and sometimes shocking experiences. Louise says she 'had a vision' she would write her own books. After her own psychic flashes combined with some gentle pressure from supportive friends, Louise decided it was the right time in her life to put her amazing story down on paper.

Angels, Demons & Me represents Louise's arrival at a point in her life where she is filled with spiritual joy having moved through a period of loss within relationships, negativity and hardship. The life experience Louise has gained shines through in her writing; the emotion and the raw sensitivity mixed in alongside a message of encouragement and a catalogue of her own Spiritual experiences.

As well as continuing her spiritual work, supported by her partner Jackie, Louise is also working on a second autobiographical book which will allow readers to gain an insight into the many life battles she endured as a child, teenager and into adulthood.

www.psychicenergyhealer.co.uk

Thank you to Tina Calder for all her hard work,
I really enjoyed working with you, you're a star x